# AMERICAN POSTERS
## OF THE TURN OF THE CENTURY

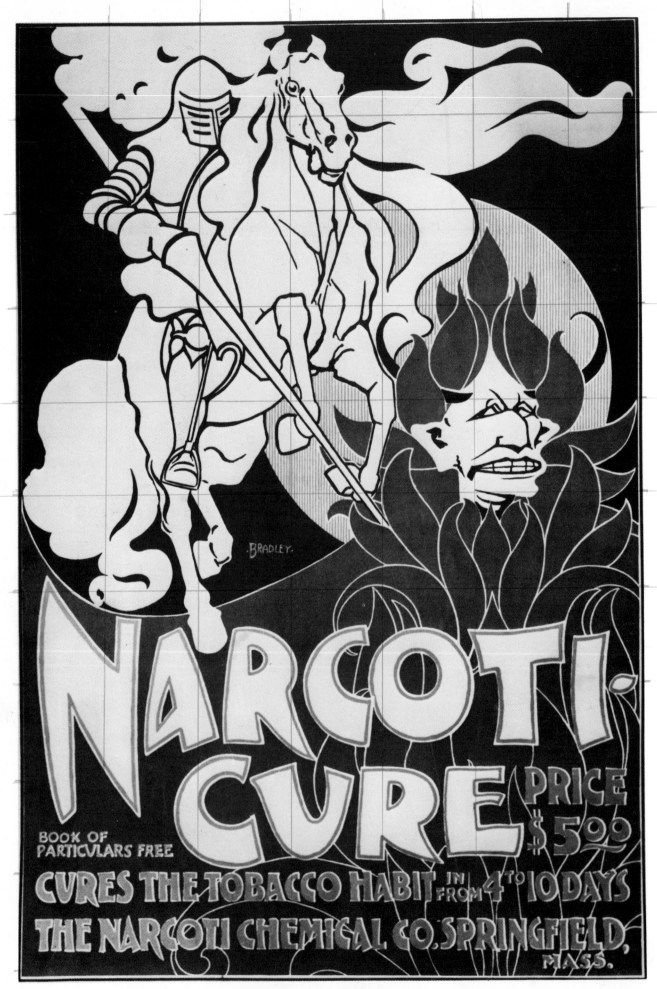

William H. Bradley  c.1895  20 x 14in

# AMERICAN POSTERS
## OF THE TURN OF THE CENTURY

# Carolyn Keay

ACADEMY EDITIONS·LONDON / ST. MARTIN'S PRESS·NEW YORK

## ACKNOWLEDGMENTS

I would like to thank the following institutions, which generously
granted permission for the reproduction of posters in their collections: the Staatsbibliothek, Berlin (pp. 37, 38, 39, 57, 75,
112); the Museum für Kunst und Gewerbe, Hamburg (p. 27); the
Hessisches Landesmuseum, Darmstadt (p. 40); the Staatsgalerie,
Stuttgart (p. 69); and the Kunsthalle, Bremen (p. 93). The staffs
of the St. Bride Printing Library of the St. Bride Institute,
London, and of the Victoria and Albert Museum, London, gave
valuable help in the research for both the articles and the illustrations in this book. Gratitude is due also to Alexander Kaspar
for his assistance in providing illustrations and to Graham Bush
for his photographs.

First published in Great Britain in 1975 by
Academy Editions 7 Holland Street London W8

SBN cloth  85670 207 2
    paper 85670 211 0

First published in the U.S.A. in 1975 by
St. Martin's Press Inc. 175 Fifth Avenue New York N.Y. 10010

Library of Congress Catalog Card Number 74-29067

Designed by Richard Kelly

Printed and bound in Great Britain by
Heffers Printers Ltd, Cambridge

# Contents

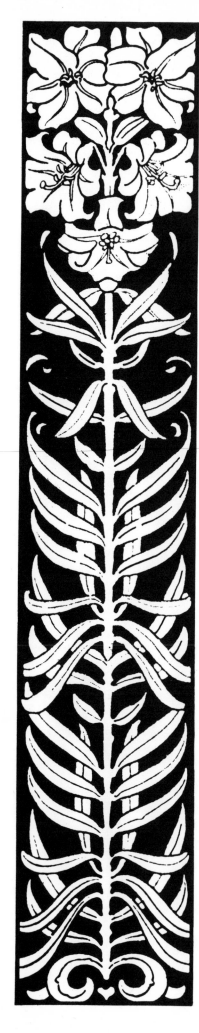

Design by Louis Rhead

Eugène Grasset

# The American Poster 1900

The poster really came into its own as an art form during the last decade of the nineteenth century. Prior to this the public had been subjected to advertisements in the form of straight letterpress posters, or of dreadful 'before and after' illustrations, or coarse reproductions of Academy paintings, the subjects of which were often totally irrelevant to the product advertised.

Suddenly the role of the poster was broadened. In addition to its primary purpose of advertising, its purely decorative qualities were realised, and the artistic poster was for the first time valued for its own sake. Huge numbers of posters were produced, often without their advertising legend, to satisfy the new demands of collectors and connoisseurs. In Europe the evolution of the poster into an aesthetic unity of design and slogan was hastened by developments in colour lithography, by the influence of the Impressionist school, and by the introduction into the West of Japanese art. Prints by Hokusai and Utamaro, newly available in London and Paris, inspired an exhilarated enthusiasm. By the 'gay nineties', the bold, colourful, joyous posters of masters like Steinlen, Bonnard, Grasset, Chéret — nicknamed by Degas 'the Watteau of the streets' — and Toulouse-Lautrec stared down from Parisian hoardings. Chéret himself was awarded the Légion d'Honneur in 1889 for the creation of a new branch of art, 'by applying art to commercial and industrial printing'. In England a long list of successful posterists was headed by the genius Aubrey Beardsley, the Beggarstaff Brothers, and Dudley Hardy. However they were all anticipated by an astonishing twenty years by Fred Walker's 1871 wood engraving for a stage adaptation of Wilkie Collins's *Woman in White,* the first poster to understand the value of solid areas of black and white. Beardsley's celebrated poster for the Avenue Theatre, designed in 1894, had a revolutionary effect on graphic art on both sides of the Atlantic, and was the most dramatic single inspiration of hundreds of American designers.

The poster craze erupted across America in the 1890s. Everywhere tremendous popular enthusiasm for decorative posters provoked endless debate on the artistic validity of the poster and its position within the echelons of fine art. Progressive museums began to form poster collections and to hold exhibitions. In Chicago it was fashionable to hold 'poster parties'. In London *The Poster,* a journal devoted exclusively to poster art, began publication in 1898, and ran for four volumes. Its pages, which treated poster art and artists with the same deference as if they were Renaissance masterpieces and Royal Academicians, are enlightening contemporary

Fred Walker 1871

records of the thriving interest generated by this new artistic medium. And publishers battened on the vogue by producing expensive limited editions, like Will Bradley's design for *The Modern Poster,* published by Charles Scribner's Sons, of which only one thousand copies were printed.

The cult was initially catalysed by a few significant influences from Europe. The most important of these were Aubrey Beardsley's decadent Art Nouveau designs, with their brilliant blending of legend and illustration. Before Beardsley, however, in 1889, Grasset executed a highly successful 'Pre-Raphaelite' illustration for *Harper's Magazine,* which was followed with a poster for the 1892 Christmas issue. In 1894 a Mr Eugene Tompkins enlivened New York with a series of Chéret posters he had bought in Paris, and which he used to publicise the revival of the play *The Old Crook.* The work of Alphonse Mucha was also known in America, although the delicate, sentimental designs of the Czech artist were not used there until the turn of the century. But there was a flourishing number of successful and gifted native artists to fulfil the demands of publishers and public, and there was no lack of work for those with talent. America had already been termed 'the promised land of advertising'. Since the Civil War she had also spawned an enormous number of journals, newspapers and magazines — of varying levels of respectability — which provided graphic artists with commissions for illustrations, covers, and publicity posters. Many of these periodicals took the form of serialised stories by popular authors, and the advertisements for them, along with publishers' posters for forthcoming book titles, make up an almost complete legacy of the contemporary literary scene. These literary posters are often the most beautiful designs of the period. Will Bradley's imaginative poster for Tom Hall's novel *When Hearts are Trumps* is a design inspired by, but not modelled on, the style of Beardsley, with its seductive curving lines, its limited colours and its pleasing harmony of illustration and lettering. Probably the first poster design of real taste and beauty to be produced in America, it is also remarkable for Bradley's technical printing skills, and helped to establish him at the beginning of a long and successful career in graphic and printing design, which ended with his post as art and typography supervisor for the Hearst film, newspaper and magazine empire.

Bradley's debt to Beardsley, though undeniable, has been unfairly exaggerated. Scotson-Clark called him 'the American B'. But one need look no further than Bradley's brilliant, often highly detailed designs for *The Chap Book* and *Victor Bicycles* to recognise the work of a highly creative and skilled artist, and along with Louis Rhead and Edward Penfield he is one of the most important designers of the time. Penfield was probably the first American artist to realise the possibilities of an aesthetic and unified design in posters, at a time when publishers were solely concerned with the practical aspects of publicity and sales promotion. His stylised, uncluttered illustrations, which clearly draw their inspiration from the Japanese print, were inventively executed in clever combinations of pen, chalk and paint, and printed in mixtures of letterpress and copper plate. His posters for *Harper's,* for whom he worked almost exclusively from 1893 to 1899, reveal a fundamental understanding of the psychology of effective publicity in their presentation of the escapist, the select, and the elegant, and are the pioneers of modern advertising.

With the Great War came a demand for a completely new type of poster, cajoling men to recruit, beseeching them to *Buy Liberty Bonds* and often working the most heart-rending and frightening sort of blackmail on the loyalties of Americans. The leading American designers of war posters were Charles Dana Gibson — best known for his creation of the 'Gibson girl' — Howard Chandler Christy, and James Montgomery Flagg, although many others, including Penfield and Maxfield Parrish, whose talents were very little suited to the task, turned to creating posters of tanks, guns and battles. For obvious reasons, the war posters are in general less attractively decorative than literary or commodity advertisements, but as posters they are no less successful. Subtlety is not one of the prerequisites of this form of art: its appeal should be spontaneous and direct, and its meaning immediately clear. The singular purpose of publicity sanctions almost any subject, and also many strange combinations of aesthetic and vulgar, which, while they may offend the purists, constitute a vital part of the life force of what Chéret termed 'The art of the street'. In spite of a certain crudeness and brashness, the potency of posters by Joseph Leyendecker and Hazel Roberts can still send a shudder down the spine.

Posters more than any other form of artistic expression are a direct reflection of their age. Although technically obsolete once their job is done, they are interesting and important as historical documents, and can be enjoyed on several levels. The works of Will Bradley, Edward Penfield, Maxfield Parrish and many other poster designers of the turn of the century provide a unique and valuable link with another culture and another time. But they also possess an intrinsic artistic merit which has too often been overlooked, and have in recent years adopted for themselves the right, previously reserved for the fine arts, to be assessed on and appreciated for their aesthetic qualities.

Carolyn Keay

## CONTEMPORARY CRITICISMS

*It is both interesting and revealing to read the reaction of contemporary art critics to the new concept of poster art. During the 1890s and the first years of the twentieth century—glorious years for the advertising poster—thousands of words were written about poster designs and their designers. The artistic qualities of the poster were discussed, methods and techniques were compared, and critics praised their favourites and condemned others with admirable partiality. On the following pages is reproduced an edited selection of articles from contemporary journals by well known critics of the time, which not only provide an insight into the new importance of tasteful and aesthetic poster design, but also illustrate the excitement and enthusiasm generated by this young and vigorous branch of art.*

# American Posters, Past and Present

H.C. BUNNER

*Scribner's Magazine*, Volume 18, October 1895

In America — at least, in the United States — the poster enjoys an absolutely unique distinction. In other countries it has been prized and admired, cherished in costly collections, and honored with the most serious artistic study and criticism. But in the United States the poster has been — and in some parts of the land it is yet — not only admired, but loved.

It was not the circus-poster that took hold on the heart of the country-folk of remote regions. Although the fondness for pictures was general in man, woman and child, it was not quite openly avowed. Certain old Puritanical traditions moved the people to look upon such home decorations as idle vanities; and even had this prejudice been less general the sources of artistic supply were meagre in the extreme. Therefore the crude and costly printed posters of the circus, the travelling juggler, the Indian herb-doctor, the horse-dealer, and, more often than the rest, the gaudy lithographs advertising agricultural implements and patent medicines, were welcomed in the little towns and at the lonely cross-roads.

Early lithographic poster drawn by Matt Morgan for the Strobridge Lithograph Company (1881)

BLACK VENUS.

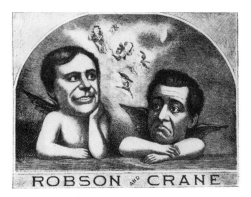

Early lithographic poster drawn by Joseph Baker for the Forbes Lithograph Company (1877)

They were not often allowed in the house; but their utilitarian character gave them a sort of right to a place on the walls of the barn; and it was here that the boys and the hired men between them would set up an art-gallery which was never quite complete until a sheet of considerable size was skilfully reft from the pictured pageant on the board fence.

The theatrical managers caught the idea; and although the establishment of the lithographic art in this country gave them facilities which they had never had before, they stuck to the primitive system of printing from roughly engraved wood-blocks, superimposing one cross-hatching of color upon another; the result attained being perhaps more hideous and incoherent than anything which could be done in any other way of color-printing.

This absurd tradition practically checked all advance in poster designing until a score of years ago; and for the most part our actors and actresses allowed themselves to be portrayed on the bill-boards in a medium so grossly and unnecessarily offensive to good taste that the meanest mountebank might have blushed to find himself so set before the world. So dead was the poster-making art that serious dramatic and lyric artists had not even the resource of tasteful and appropriate decoration for their public announcements, but were obliged to use plain type — and type of designs of half a century old. It was at this point that the Genius of Patent Medicine came to the relief of Histrionic Art.

Up to this time the Patent Medicine poster had been the most pitiful of all forms of pictorial advertising. Of these the most in use was what was known as the "Before and After" — which was short for Before and After Taking. This involved the employment of two pictures, one of which represented a lean and haggard wretch of advanced years, destitute of teeth, and but sparsely provided with hair, who was apparently trying to present his physical disabilities to the beholder in the most unpleasant possible light. The other picture showed a sturdy, lusty person in the prime of life, with well-slicked hair and as many teeth as the artist could crowd into his mouth which was always shown stretched open in a laugh of an impossibly large size. Those who gazed on this display were expected to believe that the miracle of transforming the aged wreck into an offensively healthy person of thirty-

An early confused theatrical poster designed and printed by Strobridge Lithograph Company

Wood-engraved 'stock' poster for *Rip Van Winkle,* drawn by Robert Joste

Wood-engraved 'stock' theatrical poster drawn by William H. Crane

Very coarse wood-grained theatrical poster drawn by Robert Joste for the Metropolitan Print Company

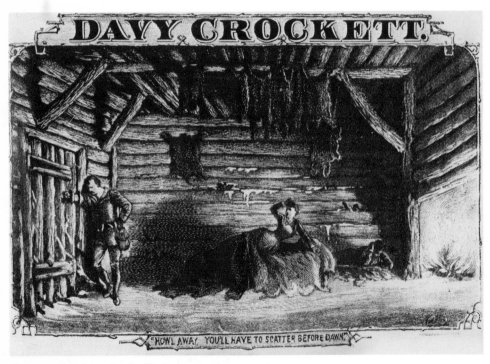

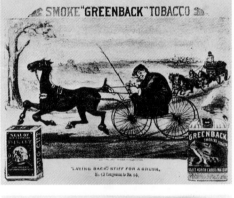

An interesting picture but ineffective poster, drawn by Matt Morgan for the Strobridge Lithograph Company

'Before and After' poster by Thomas Worth

Lithographic theatrical poster drawn by Joseph Baker (1879), for the Forbes Lithograph Company

Drawn by Hugo Zelderfield for the H.C. Miner-Springer Lithograph Company

Designed and printed by the Strobridge Lithograph Company

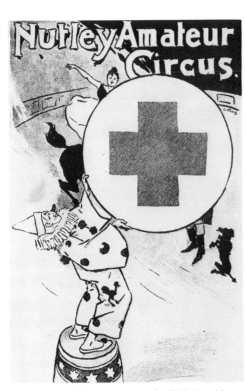

Composed and drawn on stone by F.M. Hutchins

Drawn by Robert Joste for the Metropolitan Print Company

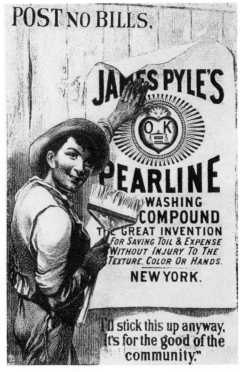

Theodore A. Liebler

F.J. Kaber

E.H. Kiefer

A.K. Moe

five had been accomplished by the use of three bottles of OLD DR. RIPLEY'S RESURGENT REINVIGORATOR OR IMBRICATED INDIAN TONIC.

But the day came when some shrewd advertiser perceived that these pictures really had no firm claim on the popular respect, and he set to work to address himself to the public, with a decent courtesy and deference. His plan worked; perhaps he surprised himself, certainly he surprised the public. Even the worried businessman, hurrying to his office, stopped when he found himself confronted with a poster that, though it bore the name of a well-known nostrum, bore also a highly attractive picture, well conceived and well executed; evidently an artist's design, and not that of an artisan; evidently made especially for the use it was put to, and evidently reproduced by the costliest skill. The success of this first appeal to the popular interest by really artistic methods was so marked and unmistakable that it found numerous imitators.

The vulgar conventionalities of the past began to lose their commercial value; and the artist was called in to do what the advertising agent had done before. But any real progress in the art of poster-making in America was checked at this time by two unfavourable circumstances. The most obvious, though the least in effect, was the fact that pictorial advertising had naturally been diverted into other channels, so that it proved cheaper and more effective to employ high-priced artists in illustrating circulars, calendars, and dainty gift-books than to set them at a somewhat discredited form of work. The second was the fact that

the German lithographer — that is, the artisan draughtsman who redraws the artist's picture upon the stone — is a man of an enduring force of character only to be found elsewhere in the mule and the martyr at the stake.

Most lithographic draughtsmen in this country are either Germans or German-Americans, and they adhere with persistence to the traditions of German technique. This technique is admirable for its purpose. The color-work is done in a highly finished crayon drawing that is really a stipple or a close imitation of it. This work takes a firm hold on stone, rendering it possible to make many prints and transfers, and by its near approach to a mechanical process bringing the work within the capacity of anybody who can learn to copy values at all.

There is no questioning the advantage of this in what is known as commercial lithography; but it makes of the lithographic workshops a very uncomfortable place for any Art that seeks a less conventional expression. The lithographic draughtsman has very little use for Art, and a profound contempt for the Artist. Set before him, at the top of his little wooden desk, the most brilliant watercolor that Fortuny ever dashed off, and as he slowly separates its mystic tints into what he considers their component elements, and reproduces them in his even, unvarying grain, that pleases him the better the more he makes it look like machine-work, he will pity the poor devil of an unskilful artist who didn't know how to finish his work up "nice and smooth."

It needs but a glance at the reproductions of the work of today that are given in these

pages to show the boldness of design and variety and novelty in technical execution have taken the place of the timorous crudity of earlier years. Unquestionably, the fact that most of our artists are still at school is quite apparent. We can forgive this when we see the American artist, consciously or unconsciously, trying to get rid of the little touch of cynical vulgarity that deforms too much of what is otherwise worthy in French art, and to keep for himself the lucid clearness and unsought force and directness of its inspiration. But imitation is not so readily forgiven when it takes the form of even a conscientious Americanization of a brutal English parody on the eccentricities of mediaeval Florentine art; and it is pleasant to see that the artist who on our side of the water has most conspicuously shown cleverness in this readaptation is growing away from his British model and developing his own characteristic powers, which point him as naturally to lines of beauty as the qualities of the foreigner urge him to a morbid delight in the contortions of ugliness.

# The Black Spot in America

**SCOTSON-CLARK**

*The Poster*, November 1900

Until the winter of 1894, the artistic poster was practically unknown in the United States. The only things of the kind, and they were very excellent and very original, were the 'Harper's Magazine' window bills by Edward Penfield. But during the latter part of 1893, and the early half of 1894, the name and work of Aubrey Beardsley had become known, and popular as was his success amongst a large class in England, his fame was tenfold in America. Every two-penny-halfpenny town had its "Beardsley Artist," and the large cities simply teemed with them. Some borrowed his ideas and adapted them to their own uses; others imitated, till one asked oneself: "Is this done by the English or American B."?

Until the introduction of the Beardsley work, all the posters seen were of the good old lithographic-printer order, where everything was stippled until all life had been taken out of it, and which at best was but the enlargement in colour of a photograph.

The first step, and a great one, was made

Will H. Bradley

by "The Century Magazine," who covered the walls of New York with what, in my humble opinion, was the best poster Grasset ever did, *i.e.*, "The Sun of Austerlitz," being Napoleon on a white horse, with a flaming background of fiery clouds. To this poster, in a great measure, was due the Napoleonic craze of the time. Next in order was Dudley Hardy's delightful "Gaiety Girl" — the dancing red girl. Napoleon looked a bit shocked when he saw her, and grieved to think that she attracted even more attention than he did, though she was turned out on two stones, while fourteen (so I was assured by the printer) were employed in his production.

Advertisers now began to see that, given an effective design, by using a few flat colours, a better result and a cheaper advertisement could be obtained. Consequently the Beardsley artist set to work.

In this line Bradley was certainly first favourite, and his output was enormous. As far as I know, he only did one large poster, an American 24-sheet Stand (28 English Double Crowns) for Frohman's production of "The Masqueraders." But he did a one-

sheet for "Hood's Sarsaparilla," which was not at all bad from an advertising point of view. Then he did several for the Chicago "Chap Book" and also for the "Inland Printer." The latter were for covers, but were also, I believe, used for posters. For mercantile houses he did several, also for his own publication, "Bradley, his Book." Clever though he undoubtedly is, I do not think he would ever have adopted the class of work in which he has become known had not Beardsley set the example. Until the latter had introduced it, people did not understand the use of the "black blot" as an element in composition. Although it had been used years before in England in the famous "Woman in White", by Fred Walker, no one seemed to realize that the solid black mass could be utilized in a decorative way.

Certainly Chicago contained the most adaptable set of men; for, starting in the new way, using only two printings, they introduced humour into their designs. First and foremost of them was Denslow, whose

Will H. Bradley

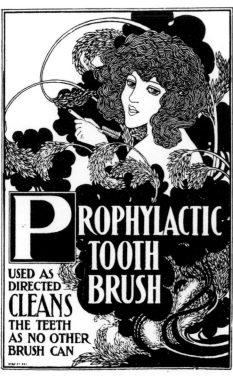

Will H. Bradley

13

"Newsboy selling a paper to a Hauti Lady" and his "Haughty Sisters" were both excellent. Denslow has, of course, been connected with journalistic art for a good many years, and though he has done some posters for the Western shows whose headquarters are in Chicago, his theatrical work did not often, as far as I know, travel east.

Bird has done some good work for magazines and so forth. His "Red Letter" window bill is, perhaps, the best known of his, but not altogether the best.

Hazenplug, unless he has done a great deal lately, is not a prolific man, but what he has done is distinctly good. "The Chap Book" poster reproduced here is excellent, and it also has the merit of having a breadth that is not discernible in some of his work.

Claude Bragdon also did a very good poster for the "Chap Book," but it was, if I remember rightly, almost entirely in outline, and the solid black was very sparingly used.

In the Far West the solid colour was employed to a fair extent. Miss Florence Lundborg who did one or two excellent posters for "The Lark", deserves all praise, for she cut her own designs on the wood block.

The first poster for "The Lark," the delightful Faun by Bruce Porter, was stencilled, and very excellent it was.

It is interesting to reproduce a design by Aubrey Beardsley, published as a window bill by the firm of Macmillan. Although it is undated, it probably appeared after his death, and I do not remember to have seen it used in England.

To see that his work had a considerable influence in America, it is only necessary to look at the cheapest form of poster work, that for the daily press. Unless I am very much mistaken, a drawing of my own,

Wilfred Denslow

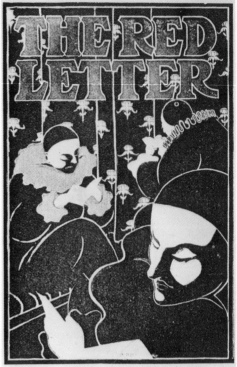

Elisha Brown Bird

reproduced by the "New York Recorder" which appeared on June 6th, 1895, was the first poster used for a daily paper. The "Chicago Times-Herald" followed two weeks afterward, having first made a bid to the "Recorder" for the use of the same drawing. This drawing was done in supposedly Beardsleyesque style. I had previously offered it to "The World", but was turned from its doors with the answer that it was "not necessary for 'The World' to use posters." Three weeks after "The Recorder" poster was published, "The World" had one, a poodle, printed in red, by De Lipmann. He did a second for the same paper and I did

Frank Hazenplug

the third. All these weekly posters were heavily plastered in solid black. We reproduce one or two by King and Outcault to give an idea as to the style of work, and to what stretches of imagination a man will allow himself to go. The poster by Mr King is not at all representative of his work. His line work, bearing in mind that it is done for cylindrical printing, is excellent. Mr Outcault, too, is better known as the inventor of "The Yellow Kid", from which series of drawings, which were started in "The World" and afterwards continued in "The Journal", gave to those two papers the title of the Yellow Press.

Among the Americans, the application of solid colour in a picture or a poster is looked upon as the invention of Beardsley. A publisher in speaking to me one day of Dudley Hardy, the Beggarstaffs, and Hassall, classed them all together as "Beardsley Artists", and when asked to explain why, the reason he gave was that they all used flat colour.

It is regrettable, but nevertheless a fact, that Beardsley unwittingly did a lot of harm. His style was easy to copy, and a great many men who had little or no knowledge of drawing were thus enabled by imitating his work to make a living, and therefore men who would otherwise have been earning an honest wage at mud-shovelling or mending the roads, were allowed to plunge into a "vortex of artistry", to cheat themselves into the belief that they were artists, and to bamboozle the man blessed with more money than taste out of his dollars.

# William H. Bradley and his Art

S.C. DE SOISSONS

*The Poster*, October 1898

The advertisement, covering any place proper for it, is one of many differences between the East and the West.

In the West the advertisement does not play any great part, and touches the people only on the surface; in the East — in the countries of feverish fight — it has entered in the blood and life, and changed the aspect of cities, towns and villages, trying to cover every inch of a free wall. Therefore, in the East also business, searching to find some new means of attracting the public attention, has employed the art; thus were originated the first artistic posters.

France, or rather Paris — *La Ville Lumière* — as a German writer, notwithstanding his Teutonic jealousy, called the "metropolis of art", started this movement, and until now is at the head of it. From Chéret — whose today already commonplace lithographs, remembering the illustrations for "petite collection Guillaume", have revolutionised a few years ago the history of the posters — to so much admired Mucha,

Will H. Bradley

of art for itself.

Herbert S. Stone, of Chicago — what a contrast, Chicago and Art! — one of the first, has not only pushed the artistic book-making, but also has brought to prominence one of the ablest poster-draughtsmen, William H. Bradley, whose five posters, made for "The Chap Book", secured for him an elevated rank among those who, by their artistic taste, have brought out the art from the museums and picture galleries into the street, before the masses, trying to elevate their taste.

Bradley's technic is different from French and English. There is a greater simplicity in the selection of colours than in French posters and he does not use as much red and black as do the English poster artists, giving thus to their work a certain monotony. In his most famous poster, which we call "The Blue", Bradley has displayed great skill by introducing the Japanese way of making pictures by a few coloured plain surfaces, such method being the source of the

France possesses a row of talented masters, who as it is always with the Frenchmen, are incomparable as far as the drawing goes.

We have there such poster-artists as Grasset, Guillaume, Toulouse-Lautrec, Boutet de Monvel, Caran d'Ache, Steinlen, and in their graceful and striking drawings we see the elegant and feverish Paris, which one can righteously call "the city of forme." In their bold, full-of-fancy works, one can see, almost always, clever masters, who can do anything with the line, because they handle it as well as they do the thought.

American artists, following closely the French art, have seized immediately the Parisian artistic fancy, have introduced it to their country and tried to "democratize" art as they do everything else, being in the meanwhile the most aristocratic country, of course in their own way.

The great publishing houses of Scribner, Harpers, The Century Co., Lippincotts, and such artistic publishers as Herbert S. Stone and Samson & Wolf contributed the most that the poster in America became — a work

Will H. Bradley

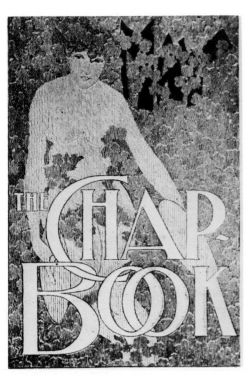

Will H. Bradley

15

direction introduced into French Art by Boutet de Monvel, and having such a strong influence on the modern illustrations and artistic posters.

In his second poster, "The Pink", he used pink, green and white — the pink being strongest and giving to his work a delicate charming effect.

The third of his "Chap Book" posters we can call "The Green", that colour prevailing; while the two last we call "The Black" and "The Red", one of them being produced by the white and black surfaces, whilst in the second there is a combination of red and black with very little white.

Bradley never repeats himself — he is different in every one of his posters. Is it a merit or a drawback? According to a certain way of reasoning it should be considered a merit, because it is proof of a great fancy of the artist, of his creative faculties, of a depth of his talent disdainful to work over the same once-found formulae. But the other theory would emphasise the strong individual stamp put on the work of an artist, as one sees it for instance in Mucha, his Byzantine style being so vigorous, that it is impossible to take his posters for another man's work.

Even Bradley's line is not always the same; sometimes it is stiff and angular, sometimes it is strong and decided, and then again delicate and winding like Oriental arabesques.

The same with his colouring. On some posters he uses large surfaces, on the other delicate spots and lines, but the result of the combination of any of three colours is quaint and artistic — sometimes it is loud, then soft.

At any rate, in our times, when there is such a great distance between useful and artistic, when the art driven out from everyday useful objects retreats more and more to the museums, and has no connection with life, the artistic posters made by Bradley are one of the links between the beautiful and the practical.

Will H. Bradley

16

# Ethel Reed and her Art

### S.C. DE SOISSONS

*The Poster*, November 1898

As in Europe, so it is in the country of the dollar, there is no lack of women artists, but there is an absolute lack of art by women, art which would express their peculiar views – which would show the feminine spirit.

It is doubtless true that this womanly way of looking at things, which is delicious if one takes it for what it is worth, has a right to be translated under an artistic form. One can understand that women have no originality of thought, and that literature and music have no feminine character, but surely women know how to observe, and what they see is quite different from that which men see, and the art which they put in their gestures, in their dresses, in the decoration of their environment, is sufficient to give us the idea of an instinctive and peculiar genius which each of them possesses.

Strictly speaking, woman only has the right to practise the system of the impressionist, she herself can limit her efforts and

Ethel Reed

translate her impressions and recompense the superficial by her incomparable charm, her fine grace, and her sweetness.

Some of them have tried to make a feminine painting. The pastels of Rosalba Carriera and the portraits of Mme. Vigée-Lebrun have some special charm in expression, design, and colouring. On the contrary, the majority of women, even the famous ones, such as Rosa Bonheur and Marie Baskirtscheff, have, one can say, a hatred for feminine visions; they make every effort to efface it from their eyes.

In the recent movement of artistic posters many women tried their powers. Conspicuous among the crowd of drawings which are without value, the work of Ethel Reed stands out for notice and high appreciation, not only because of its great artistic qualities, but because she does not take care of the intimate support things, she looks at the world as a gracious moving surface, infinitely shaded; she leaves success to itself, as if the world were a theatre of fairies, an adorable procession of passing impressions. As Edward Penfield is monopolised by Harper Bros., Gould by Lippincotts, Bradley by "The Chap Book", so Miss Ethel Reed works almost exclusively for Lamson, Wolffe and Co., of Boston. She has made seven lovely posters for that energetic and quaint-tasted publisher, only two of them having the same character, each and every one of the others is different, which fact speaks advantageously for the artist's taste. No one can accuse her of mannerisms, a very common sin among artists: even artists of great individuality.

Among half-Philistine poster collectors the most popular of Miss Reed's work is "Fairy Tales", but artistically-refined people are in ecstasies with her "Miss Traumerei", a charming combination of black, pale cream and yellow, as well as with "The White Wampum". In those two posters and in "The House of the Trees", Miss Reed uses floral motives in the same way as the Japanese, and the figures of the women created by her are as sweet, if not sweeter than the fragrant flowers surrounding them. But the best, answering its purpose of an advertising medium, is the one entitled "Is polite

society polite?" It cries loudly from afar by its glistening, warmest and most exquisite red colour one can obtain – the colour of wild poppies – a quaint design in black lines of that flower surrounding the glowing page. The same proceeding is used in "Folly or Saintliness," with the difference that the background instead of being red as in the former, is black, and the outlines of the design are of less brilliant red. Therefore the result is less effective, and more sombre.

The poster for "The Quest of the Golden Girl" is black, grey and gold, and is the least successful of Miss Reed's work, being too complicated, and in this respect resembling the plot of the novel itself.

Ethel Reed knows well the marvellous secret of design and colours, and while she

Ethel Reed

executes pictures with clever hands, she sees with her own, and not masculine eyes; her work has feminine qualities; one sees in it a woman, full of sweetness and delicacy, and this is the greatest praise one can bestow upon a woman.

Ethel Reed

Ethel Reed

Ethel Reed

# The Posters of Louis Rhead

**GLEESON WHITE**

*The Studio*, August 1896

The secret of the poster is not one to be hidden, but to be loudly proclaimed. By well placed readable lettering, and large patterns of admirably chosen colour, daring and forcible, Mr. Rhead has achieved a wide popularity that is most genuinely deserved. For if you set out to advertise certain things for sale, it is no use to do so in a modest retiring way. Audacity and arrogance befit a placard, and if the man in the street jeers at blue haired maidens, or emerald green skies, do not assume too hastily that the artist who employs them has blundered. There are many ways of attracting notice, and eccentricity is by no means a reprehensible quality in advertising. The difficulty is to be eccentric and yet to keep within the bounds of good taste. But a few years ago the damozel beloved of the Burne-Jones school would have stood no chance of finding favour in the eyes of those who advertise. Now, she is the popular heroine of the moment. That she will stay so for long is neither likely, nor entirely to be desired; but, inasmuch as the idea which governs conventional decoration is thereby advanced a step, one does not grudge her her hour of popular applause.

Mr. Rhead's work in other fields is available for reference, should any think that the simple statement of facts he deems best for a poster has been chosen to avoid the difficulties of more elaborate treatment. One has heard many an artist, before a Whistler etching or lithograph, say, "Why, I could do a dozen things like that in an hour!" For simplicity is a synonym for incompetence with those who do not realise the profound truth (paradoxical though it sound) of the epigram, "simplicity is the final refuge of the complex".

Without any wish to exalt these decorative posters beyond their intrinsic value, we may claim for them that they are novel, effective, and decorative. They have tried to embody just as much of the spirit of Pre-Raphaelite art as the hoarding can bear. Placed next to a Botticelli you would, probably, prefer the old Italian master, and one may safely say that Mr Rhead would agree with you; but to translate the spirit of the veritable Pre-Raphaelite — or his nine

teenth century disciple — to a simple phrase, easily acceptable to the people, has been Mr Rhead's purpose; and if one studies his posters with an unprejudiced mind, it is easy to admit that he has not failed. In the best there is that curious evidence of early Italy and old Japan that the very early Italian paintings bring to one's mind, as surely as does Mr. Abbey's "picture of the year" at the last Royal Academy exhibition. Japan is suggested by the colour, early Italy by the plan. The up-to-date critic cannot find adjectives sufficiently corrosive to bestow upon them. The man who has learnt to appreciate Degas and Chéret, who thinks modernity is the one valuable factor in modern art, is furious if you defend Mr. Rhead's ideal. But contemporary art is by no means all impressionism, nor all of the cockeyed primitive. There are many moods to be considered in a world of men, and he is most wise who recognises that no one creed can embrace all aspects of beauty. Now, the main purpose of

**Louis Rhead in his studio**

a poster is not to be collected, hardly to be criticised; but to arrest attention and bestow some pleasant forms and colours upon a placard when otherwise pure vulgarity would reign supreme.

Owing to the kindness of the artist we are able to reproduce some of his sketches, one showing the conception of his idea in the carefully finished study in black ink, and another from a sketch in colour. For the finished drawing Mr. Rhead submits a full size cartoon most elaborately worked up — the pigment opaque and equal, the lettering well drawn and neatly painted. Too many English artists are content to send in rough sketches and so encounter the invariable loss in their translation, besides giving the advertiser a problem which he is not always able to solve. A rough sketch in transparent washes of a set decorative pattern intended to be worked in solid flat colour, much as it may appeal to a fellow artist, is apt to look merely untidy to the average man; and the

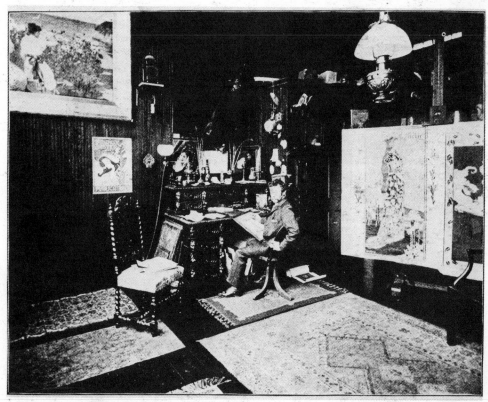

19

juicy, broken colour that is so attractive to painters not merely fails to charm him, but is positively misleading, since it really represents a quality that no chromo-lithograph can reproduce accurately. When you see a poster of Mr. Rhead's in the original, and the proof side by side with it, it is not easy at first sight to determine which is the autograph; and this is as it should be, because it proves that the designer has fully understood the limits of his material.

The following is a complete list of the posters designed by Louis J. Rhead, up to January, 1896:

For HARPER'S BAZAAR: *Easter,* 1890. "Daffodils" in yellow, green, and red; *Thanksgiving,* 1891. "Figure of Plenty" in red, brown, on yellow paper; *Thanksgiving,* 1892; the same design, but the figure replaced by naturalistic picture, and border in pink, and dark brown; *Christmas,* 1892. The same with border of green mistletoe, panel changed to naturalistic picture; *Thanksgiving,* 1894. "Girl with fruit" in green, red, and purple; *Christmas,* 1894. "Girl in snow" in red, green, brown and grey; For HARPER'S MAGAZINE: November, 1891. "Fame", five figures, in red and black; *Christmas* 1891. "Puritan maid with mistletoe" in green, red, and green; CENTURY MAGAZINE: *Christmas,* 1891. "Literature and Art" in red and black; *Christmas,* 1892. "Bells" in red, and green, on green; *Christmas,* 1894. "Girl with peacock" in green, yellow, blue, two sizes; *Midsummer,* 1894. "Reading girl" in white, blue red, green; *Christmas,* 1895. "Father Christmas, carrying plum pudding", in

Design for a poster by Louis Rhead

orange, red, green, two sizes; *Midsummer,* 1895. "Girl with fan", yellow sunflowers. ST. NICHOLAS: May, 1892. "Children dancing round Maypole. Spring blossoms", in red, blue, green, yellow; *August,* 1892. "Mermaid in the sea" in blue, purple, and red; *August,* 1894. "Child with dogs" in red, blue, and brown; *Christmas,* 1894. "St Nicholas with holly branch" in blue, orange, and red; *Christmas,* 1895. Border, books and holly, centre panel of children cut out.

Besides these there are: *D. Appleton's list of holiday books, Christmas,* 1891, in red and black; *Ladies' Home Journal, January,* 1893. Brown border on cream paper; *Great Men and famous Women,* in brown on green; *Royal Baking Powder, cook book,* "Girl holding cake" in red, purple, green, and blue; *Cycle Cigarettes,* in red, yellow, blue, and purple; *Calendar Photochrome Engraving Co.,* "Girl painting" in pink, purple, yellow, and green; *Pyle's Pearline,* "Girl hanging out clothes" in dress green and red, lilies below; *Girl washing,* in red, purple, green and yellow; "Dancing girls holding package of pearline" in red, blue, green, and yellow; *Lundborg's Perfumes:* "Seated Girl" in red hair, pink blossoms on yellow ground; *Girl scattering violets* in purple and yellow; *Girl in pink* in black hair, green plants; *Prang's Poster Calendar.* "Girl in yellow", *Holiday Publications.* "Girl in purple", *Easter Publications.* "Angel with lilies" in gold, red and purple. Also posters for *Devil and Deep Sea,* by Kipling; *Winter tales for winter nights;* girl in red, green and purple; *How the brigadier played for a kingdom;* figure on white horse. *Winter Clothing,* man in overcoat, snow on ground. *Cover for Easter newspaper.* Angel with lilies, and daffodil border; and *The Bookman,*

*Christmas,* 1895, in black, yellow, green; *Scribner's Magazine,* 1895. "Girl with mistletoe" in woods, snow on ground; *N.Y. Herald,* Christmas 1895. "Father Christmas, with boar's head", figure in red; and others; theatrical poster for Richard Mansfield's *Comedy and Tragedy,* and one for Holland Brothers; figures of drama in red, with masks.

The series best known on this side for *The Sun* (New York) include: *Girl in Crimson Robe,* blue road, yellow sky; *Girl in Red,* holding sun, rays in yellow, blue background; *Girl in Black,* orange sun, green fields, with purple grapes; *Girl in Purple,* with children receiving presents; Christmas, *Girl in Red,* skating; and *Girl in Blue,* walking on snow, purple trees, yellow sky.

Those for the *Journal* (New York) include: *Two Standing Figures,* in red, orange, purple, blue, rooster crowing: *Two Seated Figures,* in blue, yellow, green, and purple; and *Figure in Chariot,* white horses, gold sun, yellow clouds. To these one must add, *King's Malt Extract* (Boston), Girl in Indian red, holding grain, windmill in distance; *Rickseker's Perfumes* (New York), Girl in boat, blue, yellow, green, red; *Packer's Tar Soap,* Girl holding her hair, which is crowned with pine cones; *Meadow Grass,* green and gold; and *Copco Soap,* girl in white at the bath, blue, red, purple, yellow, with about thirty other designs which have been executed for various houses, and many other schemes which will soon be seen on both sides of the ocean, but not yet issued.

At the show of Mr. Rhead's work were two panels, the one, white swans on a blue and green background, the other, peacocks, which the artist intends, I believe, for tapestry weaving. Their delightful colour, a rich harmony of peacock-blues, greens and purples, could not be effectively reproduced here, but they rivalled a stained glass window in their gorgeous harmonies.

Design for a poster by Louis Rhead

Design for a poster by Louis Rhead

Louis Rhead

Louis Rhead

# Pictorial Book Advertisements in America

## CHARLES HIATT

*The Poster and Art Collector*, Volume VI

### I – Some Designs by Maxfield Parrish

The great charm of Mr. Parrish's work lies in its curious individuality. It may well be said that he has felt the influence of many predecessors in design, but his work is stamped with his own originality. He is adroit enough effectively to conceal his borrowings if indeed he has borrowed at all. He realises for us a fairyland, undiscovered until he became its pioneer. For the most part his fairy pictures are less obtrusively fantastic than those of the older artists. Every fact in the picture in itself appears to be tangible: it is the atmosphere with which Mr. Parrish invests all his facts which produces the sense of aloofness and elusiveness which one feels as one looks at his drawings.

I should think that the violent contrasts of primary colours were difficult to a man of Mr. Parrish's temperament. As a rule his colour schemes are low and subdued. Silvery greys, dull greens and reds, yellows and

Maxfield Parrish

NO GENTLEMAN OF FRANCE
THE MASK AND WIG CLUB
UNIVERSITY OF PENNSYLVANIA

Maxfield Parrish

browns are the hues which he most often affects. He is skilful in manipulating flat tints without producing a dull flat effect. His detail is complicated, but the net impression is by no means restless or confused. Nobody knows better than he how to fill in the middle distance with a pleasant little landscape with re-roofed cottages or the like which give a touch of human interest to his often fantastic patterns. He is careful to leave no part of his design without definite meaning and interest, and his lettering is both well drawn and admirably displayed. Of the four bills reproduced here, the colour scheme of that for the "Century Midsummer Holiday Number" is perhaps the most striking. The paper is yellow, the foliage of the trees blue-green and their trunks are almost violet. The nude figure of warm brown with black hair sits in a field of vivid

green grass. Artistically, the bill for "Scribner's Fiction Number" is perhaps more satisfactory. The predominant colours are grey, dull brown, and slate blue. In the "Harper's Weekly: National Authority on Amateur Sport" placard, the figures of the three golfers are almost photographic in their realism. The undulating landscape, with its trees and cottage in the middle distance, is quite delightful. The very small advertisement for "No Gentleman of France: The Mask and Wig Club, University of Pennsylvania", shows Maxfield Parrish in a very different mood. The grotesque soldier on horseback, the parade of decorative heraldry, the simple colour scheme of black, white, bright red and pale blue, make up an effective whole.

### II – Some Bills by Will Carqueville

Without claiming for them the same impor-

Maxfield Parrish

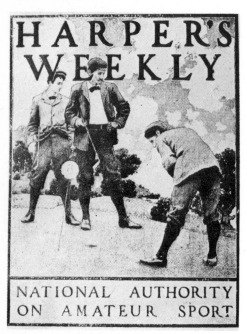

Maxfield Parrish

Will Carqueville

tance as the memorable advertisements of Mr. Penfield, it seems to me that the window bills of Mr. Will Carqueville are less well-known in England than they deserve. Mr. La Fogue, writing in 1897 in that sumptuous and inaccessible work *Les Affiches Etrangères,* tells us: "La direction de 'Lippincott's Magazine' a employé comme dessinateur pour ses affiches M. Will Carqueville. Nous rencontrons là tous les sujets habituels, s'appliquant aux mois, aux saisons, aux journées commémoratives. Arrêtons-nous aux données les plus

originales. Voici d'abord le mois d'Avril: trois demoiselles épellant en commun le titre de 'Lippincott's Magazine'. Elle se ressemblent tellement, avec leur petit nez retroussé, que maman a eu soin, pour s'y reconnaître, de teindre leur chevelure en rouge, noir et jaune, repectivement. Le fond du tableau est vert olive et les profils sont d'une paleur à rendre jaloux le plus candide des pierrots. Le mois de Mai nous ramène à la prairie en fleur. Une jeune fille s'approche d'un arbuste pour cueillir une rose trémière; elle a soin, d'un geste rapide, de garantir sa

robe blanche du contact avec un gazon fraîchement peint en vert, ce qui doit la mettre en état de soutenir la lutte contre l'outremer intense du ciel." I reproduce two of the placards described by Mr. La Fogue in illustration of this brief note. Of them the more effective is the "Lippincott's May", in which the effective juxtaposition of bright contrasting colours produces an effect of gaiety similar to that of a haphazard nosegay of country flowers. The "Lippincott's April" is very effective. According to Mr. La Fogue, the mother of the three girls who are devouring the contents of the magazine would have great difficulty in distinguishing her daughters one from the other, were it not that one has scarlet hair, a second black hair, and a third yellow hair. It is a pity that most of the designs for Lippincott's include a realistic representation of the magazine itself. In the example before us the cover is reproduced so that the contents may be read although they are printed in small type. I do not think that this in any way increases the value of the bill as an advertisement, while on the other hand, it not unfrequently takes much from the beauty of the design. This drawback is not felt in Mr. Carqueville's charming little placard for the June issue. A girl in black dress and red striped blouse is represented lazily angling from a punt moored in a backwater amidst water-lilies and tall sword-like rushes. The inevitable magazine lies open, *face downwards* (shame, O fair barbarian!) on the seat in front. The green of the prairie and the blue of the sky produce a vivid contrast, and the bright red lettering is displayed with great effect. Mr Carqueville has been successful in achieving a glow of colour wholly devoid of rawness. At the International Advertisers' Exhibition held at the Crystal Palace last summer, several of this artist's advertisements for "Lippincott's Magazine", and one for "Lippincott's Select Novels" were shown together, and made one of the best pieces of decoration in the American section. The bill for the "International: April" depends more for its effect on colour than on design, and to its brilliant and victorious colour a reproduction in half-tone of necessity does scant justice. It emphasises the artist's skill in

making vehement colour contrasts without producing the crude and brutal results with which in England we are only too familiar.

III – Some Designs by J. J. Gould

Mr. Gould would seem to be placard-designer in ordinary to that excellent periodical "Lippincott's Magazine". During the year 1896, he did twelve distinct designs, that is to say, a new one for each issue of the publication. All of these, together with two or three other examples of his work, were shown at the International Advertisers' Exhibition held at the Crystal Palace last May. I do not wish in the smallest degree to offend Mr. Gould when I say that my pleasure in his designs would be ten times as great as it is, if I had not seen those of Mr. Penfield. When I state that I know absolutely nothing of Mr. Gould's work apart from his posters, and that I have no idea of his age, I trust that I shall not be understood to mean that his work is an imitation of that of Mr. Penfield. It is possible that Mr. Gould was first in the field and that the merit of establishing a singularly effective convention properly belongs to him. It is certain that the convention of both these artists is almost identical, and I venture to believe that Mr. Penfield is altogether more felicitous in his employment of it than Mr. Gould. The colour schemes of both these artists are simple and brilliant without a suspicion of that rawness which comes of the unskilful contrast of large masses of primary colours.

They achieve emphasis without brutality; their bills are so innocent of vulgarity that they pleasantly adorn the walls of a living

room. Like Mr. Penfield, Mr. Gould understands the art of making a striking pattern – his placing is almost always good. His lettering is well-drawn and forms, as it should form, an essential part of the pattern. Into the Lippincott series of bills Mr. Gould always introduces a realistic representation of the magazine itself. For this he should not be blamed, for doubtless the publishers insist on it. As I noted last month, Mr. Maxfield Parrish and Mr. Will Carqueville seem to have suffered from the same futile obligation.

As a draughtsman Mr. Gould is markedly

J.J. Gould

Will Carqueville

J.J. Gould

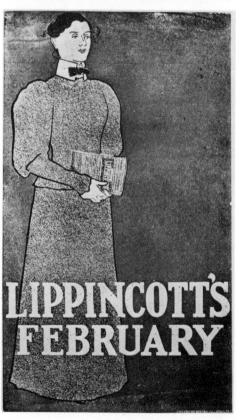

inferior to Mr. Penfield. There is in all the work of the latter a suggestion of reserved force, and amazing vigour, which is as a rule absent from Mr. Gould's productions. Mr. Gould has caught something of the manner of Mr. Penfield, something of his simplicity and directness, but he falls far short of him in strength and impressiveness. The bills for the February, July and November issues of Lippincott's, which are reproduced here, bear a distinct general likeness to the productions of Mr. Penfield. When I say this, I am far from making any suggestion of unworthy or illegitimate imitation. The abilities of Mr. Gould render such imitation entirely unnecessary. At the same time I could wish for greater individuality, a less obvious indication of the source of derivation. In the "Lippincott's July", Mr. Gould is more himself. The colour-scheme of vivid crimson, bright green, and dull brown is a happy one, and the composition is as simple as it is effective.

IV – Some designs by Florence Lundborg

It is to Miss Florence Lundborg, of San Francisco, that we owe the most interesting of the placards designed for *The Lark*. The lady cut her designs on the wood block herself, so that they have an altogether exceptional value. The effects attempted are of the simplest character. The pattern is of the boldest, reminding one of the naive chap-book ornaments of other days, or of the designs in chap-book style made by Joseph Crawhall. These quaint and simple

Florence Lundborg

things, touched as they are with the archaic, are very welcome amidst the smooth and over – finished productions which American lithographers turn out. They have more of the personality of their inventor than the mechanically produced lithograph can possibly have. At all events they were exactly the right things with which to announce the issues of such a journal as *The Lark*. Miss Lundborg's placards are dated May, August and November, 1895, and February, August and November, 1896. One of the best is that in which a little child, pointing to a bird flapping its wings, asks its mother: 'What is that?' and receives the reply: 'That is *The Lark* appearing.' The two designs which we reproduce are typical of a series which is in many ways unique. A complete set of *The Lark* advertisements is a very desirable possession. As the largest of them measures little more than eighteen inches by twelve, they can be kept in a portfolio of moderate dimensions. From the collector's point of view, American book advertisements are ideal in that they nearly all are of small size and are printed on good paper....

VII – Some Bills by George Wharton Edwards

Mr. George Wharton Edwards is among the most distinguished and prolific, if he is not one of the most original, living decorative pen draughtsmen of America. His book decorations have won for him a very conspicuous place in a country in which the decoration of books employs the talents of many brilliant artists. Mr. Wharton Edwards was born in New York, but came to Europe in order to study art. He has made a speciality of Dutch landscape and fisher-

George Wharton Edwards

folk, and he has spent much time in Brittany. The bill for *The Century Magazine* (September, 1896), which we reproduce here, is a pleasant thing in grey, the lettering being in brown. Mr. Wharton Edwards has also designed posters for the February, March, April, May, and September issues of *The Century* (1895). The last is, perhaps, the best known and most successful of his placards. It represents a woman with an enigmatical smile, in flowing classic costume, seated at the foot of a Corinthian column. In the foreground are a group of poppies and a fountain. Among Mr. Wharton Edwards's other posters is one for the December number of *St. Nicholas* (1894); another for *The Man who Married the Moon;* and a third for the May number of *The Bookman* (1897). The last is printed in black on a yellow ground, the long cloaked figure of the man being in silhouette. He wears a red cap, which forms the only patch of colour in the whole composition.

Nearly all the placards designed by Mr. Wharton Edwards fulfil their purpose well. He certainly exhibits great versatility in the making of them. Nobody could possibly accuse him of being the slave of a single style. Indeed, he is so various that his work cannot be said to be characterised by any marked individuality, but it is always agreeable, and sometimes really accomplished.

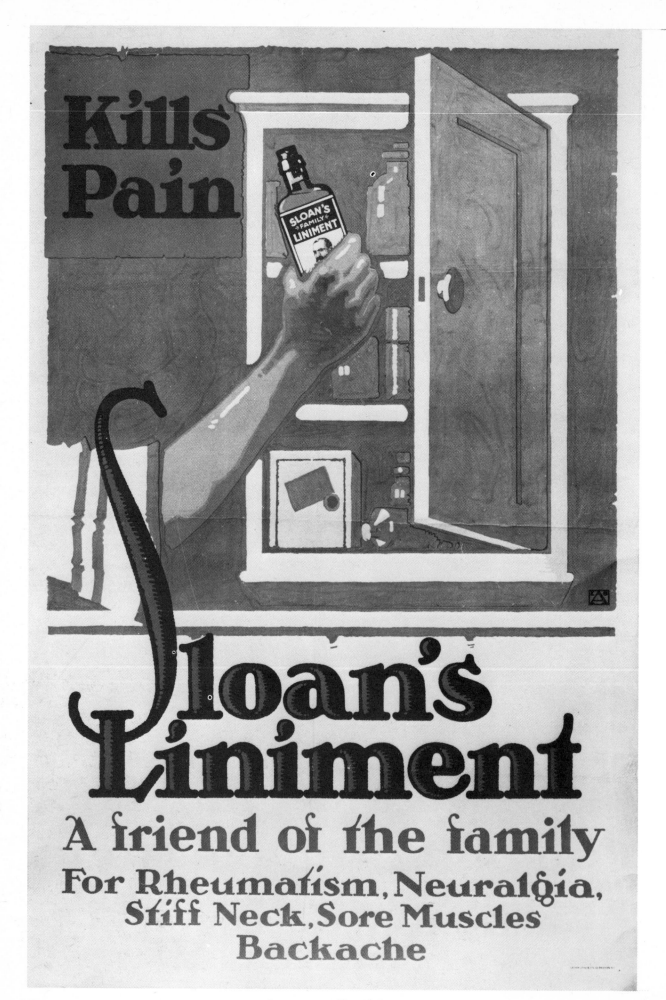

Anonymous  45 x 30.5in

26

# Biographical
# Notes

**Elisha Brown Bird** *b. 1867*
Born in Boston, Massachusetts, Bird was a designer of posters for *The Chap-Book* and *The Century*. He also contributed to the journals of the *Inland Printer, The Chap-Book* and *The Red Letter.*

**William H. Bradley** *10.7.1868 – 25.1.1962*
Posterist, illustrator, publisher, and printer, Will Bradley was nicknamed 'the American B' by Scotson-Clark, because of the influence of Aubrey Beardsley on his work. He was born in Boston, and at an early age received drawing lessons from his father, who was a cartoonist for the *Daily Item* of Lynn, Massachusetts. In 1880 he began a long career in printing in a 3-dollars-a-

week job as a printer's devil with *The Iron Agitator,* and in 1887 moved to Chicago as a fully-fledged designer with the prestigious printers Knight and Leonard. He rented a studio and began taking in freelance work, and by the 90s was one of the most sought-after designers in America. On the strength of his poster and illustrations for *When Hearts are Trumps* by Tom Hall, a series of covers for *The Inland Printer,* and a theatre poster for *The Masqueraders,* he received marvellous commissions from *Harper's Weekly, Harper's Bazaar* and *Harper's Young People.* In 1895 he opened the Wayside Press in Springfield, Boston, and began publication of *Bradley: His Book, a Monthly Magazine, Devoted to Art, Literature and Printing,* for which he was editor, poet, artist, art critic, designer and printer-publisher in one. This work, however, was soon too demanding on his time: the business was taken over by the University Press, Boston, and Bradley opened a design and art service in New York, specialising in bicycle catalogues. He later moved on to become art director of several leading American journals, including *Collier's Magazine, Good Housekeeping, Metropolitan, The Century,* and

William H. Bradley  14 x 10in

William H. Bradley  c.1896  19.5 x 8.5in

William H. Bradley  1895  20 x 12in

*Pearson's.* He wrote and illustrated a children's book *Peter Poodle, Toy Maker to the King,* and a novel *Castle Perilous,* which was serialised and illustrated by him in *Collier's.* From 1915 to 1917 he worked as art supervisor for a series of films for William Randolph Hearst. He then turned to writing and directing films, and in 1920 was appointed art and typography supervisor for Hearst magazines, newspapers and films. In 1955 he published his autobiography under the title *Will Bradley: His Chap Book.* He died in La Mesa, California, in 1962, at the age of 94.

### Claude Fayette Bragdon *1866 – 17.9.1946*
Born in Oberlin, Ohio, Bragdon studied in Buffalo under Bruce Price, von Green and Wicks. As well as working as an architect and illustrator, he designed furniture, book jackets, ornaments and posters, and was the author of a work entitled *The Beautiful Necessity.* Among his successful architectural projects were the Genessee Valley Club, Rochester, and the law courts in Genessee, New York. He was a contributor to *The Chap-Book, Scribner's Magazine* and *Life,* and designed posters for many magazines and for the newspaper *The Rochester Post Express.* He died in New York City in 1946.

### Charles Livingston Bull *1874 – 22.3.1932*
Born in New York State and ended his life in Oradell, New Jersey. He was a painter of animals and illustrator, and belonged to both the New York Watercolour Club and the Society of Illustrators. Books which he illustrated include *Call of the Wild, Watchers of the Trails,* and *Kindred of the Wild,* and he was the author of *Under the Roof of the Jungle,* 1911.

### Blendon Reed Campbell *b. 28.7.1872*
Born in St. Louis, Missouri, and studied in Paris under Whistler, Laurens and Benjamin Constant. Campbell became a member of the American Art Association in Paris and the Society of Illustrators in New York, and in the years immediately before and after 1900 was a poster designer for *Scribner's Magazine.*

### William L. Carqueville *1871 – 14.8.1946*
Apart from some time spent studying in Paris, Will Carqueville lived all his life in Chicago, where he founded a lithographic press. Although he was also a painter and draughtsman, he concentrated mainly on designing posters for *Lippincott's,* and it is for these that he is best known. His themes and subjects are reminiscent of the designs of Edward Penfield.

### Howard Chandler Christy *10.1.1873 – 4.3.1952*
Although best known for his book illustrations, Christy was also a popular portrait painter. He studied at the Academy and Art Students League, New York, before departing for the Spanish American War. His illustrated accounts of the war were published in *Scribner's,*

*Harper's* and *Collier's Weekly,* and he was one of the leading poster designers of the First World War. An exhibition of his work was held in the Ainsmie Gallery, New York in 1922. There is a large painting by him, entitled *Signity of the Constitution,* in the Capitol, Washington DC.

### George Wharton Edwards *14.3.1869 – 18.1.1950*
Painter, designer, illustrator and author. Born in Fairhaven, Connecticut, and studied in Antwerp and Paris. Works illustrated by Edwards include Austin Dobson's *Sun Dial,* and *Old English Ballads,* and he designed posters for *The Century* and for the Twenty-eighth Exhibition of the American Watercolor Society. His literary publications, many of which are illustrated with coloured reproductions of his own paintings, include *Vanished Towers and Climes of Flanders, Holland of Today,* and *Belgium Old and New.* He died in Greenwich, Connecticut.

### Charles Dana Gibson *14.9.1867 – 23.12.1944*
Born in Roxbury, Massachusetts, Gibson was the best known of the American wartime poster designers and

Frank Hazenplug c.1896 20.5 x 13.5in

had considerable influence on other American and European illustrators. He became famous as the creator of the 'Gibson Girl', a modern American young lady who appeared in his posters, designs and illustrations. He was a student with the Art Students League, New York in 1884–85 and later studied in Paris (1893–94). He worked as an illustrator for various New York magazines, in particular *Scribner's* and *Harper's,* and for the *Pall Mall Magazine* in London, and then successfully published collections of his magazine illustrations under titles such as *The American Girl Abroad, Drawings – Humorous American Pictures, Pictures of People* and *People of Dickens.* Books illustrated by Gibson include Hope's *The Prisoner of Zenda* and *Rupert of Hentzau* and Magruder's *The Violet.* He died in New York City in 1944.

### J.J. Gould
One of the best known poster designers of his time, although like Will Carqueville he worked almost exclusively for *Lippincott's* in Philadelphia. There are two signatures: J.J. GOULD and J.J. GOULD JR.

### Frank Hazenplug *b. 1873*
Born in Dixon, Illinois, Hazenplug was a student at the Chicago School of Art. A painter and illustrator, he was best known for his posters and illustrations for the magazine *The Chap-Book.* He also designed for *Living Posters.* The influence of Will Bradley is much in evidence in his work.

### Joseph Christian Leyendecker *23.5.1874 – 25.7.1951*
Leyendecker was born in Montabaur, Eifel, of German parentage, and emigrated to America, where he made his home. He studied at the Art Institute of Chicago and the Académie Julian in Paris, and worked as an illustrator and poster designer, contributing mainly to the magazines *The Interior, The Century, The Inland Printer* and *Art in Dress.* In 1895 his poster for the August Midsummer Holiday Number of *The Century* gained first prize in a competition which attracted 700 entries.

### Florence Lundborg *1871 – 18.1.1949*
Born in San Francisco, Florence Lundborg studied in France and Italy and at the Mark Hopkins Institute of Art, and became a member of the National Association of Women Painters and the San Francisco Art Association. She was a well-known artist, illustrator, and poster designer, and executed murals in the California Building of the Panama Pacific Exhibition, the Metropolitan Museum, the Wadleigh High School, New York, and the Shallow High School, Brooklyn. Her book illustrations include *The Rubayat, Yosemite Legends* and *Odes and Sonnets.* The woodcuts she designed for the posters advertising *The Lark* were cut by the artist herself.

### Henry McCarter *5.7.1866 – 20.11.1942*
An artist and illustrator who studied in Philadelphia and also in Paris under Puvis de Chavannes, Bonnat and Toulouse-Lautrec, Henry McCarter contributed to *Scribner's, The Century, Collier's* and in particular *Harper's,* and gained many awards, including the gold medal for illustration at the Panama Pacific Exhibition, San Francisco, in 1915. McCarter was a teacher at the Academy of Fine Arts, Philadelphia, and the Art Students League, New York. His work shows the marked influence of Will Bradley and of Japanese art.

### Blanche McManus (Mrs Francis Milton Mansfield) *b. 2.2.1870*
Born in Louisiana, Blanche McManus studied in Paris, where she eventually made her home. Although primarily a book and magazine illustrator, she designed some successful posters, including *The Adventures of Captain Horn* and *The True Mother Goose.* She was also the author of *The American Woman Abroad* and *Our French Cousins.*

Florence Lundborg c.1895  16.5 x 10in

**Maxfield Parrish** *25.7.1870 – 30.3.1966.*
Parrish excelled as a book illustrator although he was also a successful poster designer. The son of Stephen Parrish, the painter and etcher, he was born in Philadelphia. He studied first at Haverford College, spent three years at the Pennsylvania Academy of Fine Arts, and then worked under Harold Pyle at the Drexel Institute. He designed posters for the Adlake camera, *Scribner's Magazine, Collier's* and *The Century,* and illustrated Kenneth Grahame's *The Golden Age, Mother Goose in Prose,* and *Poems of Childhood.* In 1906 he became a member of the National Academy of Design, New York, and his work was shown at the Paris Exhibition of 1900 and the Pan-American Exhibition, Buffalo, 1901.

**Edward Penfield** *2.6.1866 – 8.2.1925*
Edward Penfield was born in Brooklyn. Along with Rhead and Bradley, he was one of the most successful American poster designers of his time, and was also one of the first artists to work in this field. From 1891 to 1901 he worked as director with Harper and Brothers, New York, and originally became known for his series of poster designs for *Harper's Magazine,* although he later designed numerous posters for *Collier's* and for forthcoming book titles. Among the best known of these are *Three Gringos in Central America and Venezuela* and *On Snow Shoes to the Barren Grounds.* He also illustrated magazine articles, and after visits to Holland and Spain, he published his own illustrated impressions, *Holland Sketches* (1907) and *Spanish Sketches* (1911), originally as magazine articles and then in book form. He was, in addition, a successful mural artist, decorating the break-

fast room of Randolph Hall, Cambridge, and the living room of a country club in Rochester. He died in Beacon, New York.

**Edward Henry Potthast** *10.6.1857 – 10.3.1927*
Born in Cincinnati, where he studied at the Academy, as well as in Paris, Munich and Antwerp. Most of Potthast's poster designs were for the theatre and circus, although he also executed one to advertise *The Century.* He was a member of the National Academy of New York.

**James Preston** *1874 – 15.1.1962*
Preston was a landscape painter and book illustrator, and much of his best work was done in the field of book illustration, ex libris plates and book jackets. In 1915 he exhibited in the Pennsylvania Academy of Fine Arts, Philadelphia. He was married to Mary Wilson, the illustrator, and lived in New York.

**Ethel Reed** *b. 1876*
Born at Newburyport, Massachusetts. By the age of eighteen she was well-known for her book illustrations, and her reputation was soon increased by her poster designs. She was also an artist and cartoonist. She received much of her training from the miniaturist Laura

Sheridan 1918 26 x 18.5in

Edward Penfield 25.5 x 20.5in

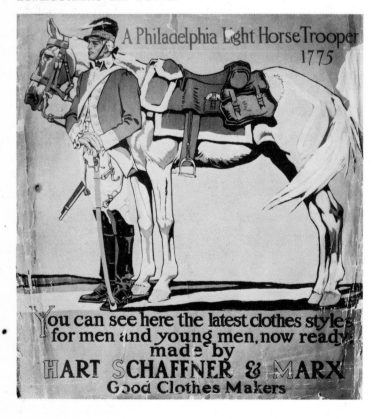

Hill. Among her many published designs were a series of groups of children reminiscent of Kate Greenaway, illustrations, also of children, to the poems of Louise Chandler Moulten, and contributions to the magazine *Punch*. Her posters, of which the most famous are *The Arabella and Araminta Stories, Miss Träumerei* and *The House of Trees* by Ethelwyn Wetherald, depict outdoor rustic scenes. She came to work almost exclusively for Lamson, Wolffe and Company in Boston, where she lived.

## Louis J. Rhead *6.11.1857 – 29.7.1926*
Rhead was an Englishman born in Wedgwood's Etruria, Staffordshire. His father was an artist at the pottery factory, his brother a member of the English Society of Painter-Etchers. At the age of thirteen he went to Paris to study under Boulanger, and then entered the School at South Kensington, studying under Poynter and Leighton. After working as a designer of book jackets and posters for *Cassell's Magazine*, he was invited to America by D. Appleton & Co., publishers, and eventually settled there. On a visit to Paris he made the acquaintance of Grasset, an event which fostered his interest in posters. He exhibited posters in New York (1896) and Paris (1897), and was awarded gold medals at a poster exhibition in Boston and the 1904 World Exhibition at St. Louis in 1904. Rhead also did some designs for interiors, and illustrated books, newspapers and magazines. He was the author of three books: *A Book of Fish and Fishing, American Front Stream Insects,* and *Fisherman's Lures*.

## John Sloan *2.8.1871 – 7.9.1951*
Born at Lockhaven, Philadelphia, of Irish parentage, Sloan studied at the Pennsylvania Academy, Philadelphia. An artist, illustrator, caricaturist and etcher, he began his career as an illustrator for the Philadelphia *Press* and *Enquirer*, and then worked in New York for *Everybody's Magazine, Harper's* and *Collier's Weekly*. He taught at the Art Students League and in 1931 became its director. His work reveals above all the influences of Toulouse-Lautrec, Steinlen and Aubrey Beardsley. He was one of the original members of the group of artists known as 'The Eight', who were influential in promoting modern realism in the U.S.A. He gained the bronze medal for his etchings at the Panama-Pacific Exhibition, San Francisco (1915), and in 1950 won the gold medal from the American Academy of Arts, New York. He is probably best known for his depiction of human scenes in the Lower East Side, the Bowery and West Greenwich Village sections of New York.

## Albert Edward Sterner *8.3.1863 – 16.12.1946*
Born in London, Sterner studied at the Académie Julian and the Ecole des Beaux Arts in Paris before emigrating to America in 1879. A painter, illustrator and lithographer, he worked in New York as an illustrator of books and for the magazine *Life*. He taught at the Art Students League and was one of the founders of the Society of Illustrators. In 1910 he became a member of the National Academy, and in 1918 President of the Painter-Gravers of America.

## Robert J. Wildhack *b. 27.8.1881*
Born in Illinois, Wildhack was a painter and illustrator who had studied under Robert Henri in New York. He worked primarily as a designer of posters for books and magazines.

## Charles Herbert Woodbury *14.7.1864 – 21.1.1940*
Woodbury was a seascape painter, etcher and posterist from Massachusetts. He studied at the Massachusetts Institute of Technology and at the Académie Julian in Paris, and later became President of the Boston Water-color Club. He took gold medals for oil painting at the Atlanta Exposition, 1895, and the Panama-Pacific Exposition, San Francisco, 1915, and was author of *Paintings and the Personal Equation* and *The Art of Seeing*.

Adolph Theidler 1916 38.5 x 19.5in

# THE
# POSTERS

Elisha Brown Bird  c.1896  20.5 x 13.5in

Elisha Brown Bird  26.5 x 14.5in

William H. Bradley  c.1895  20.5 x 14in

35

William H. Bradley  c.1902  19 x 14in

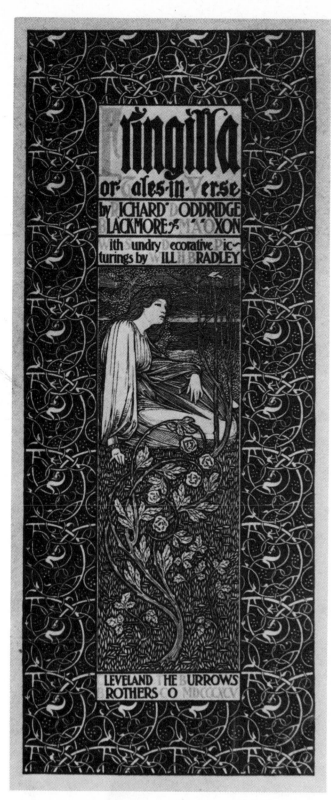

William H. Bradley 1895 21 x 10in

William H. Bradley c.1896 20 x 9.5in

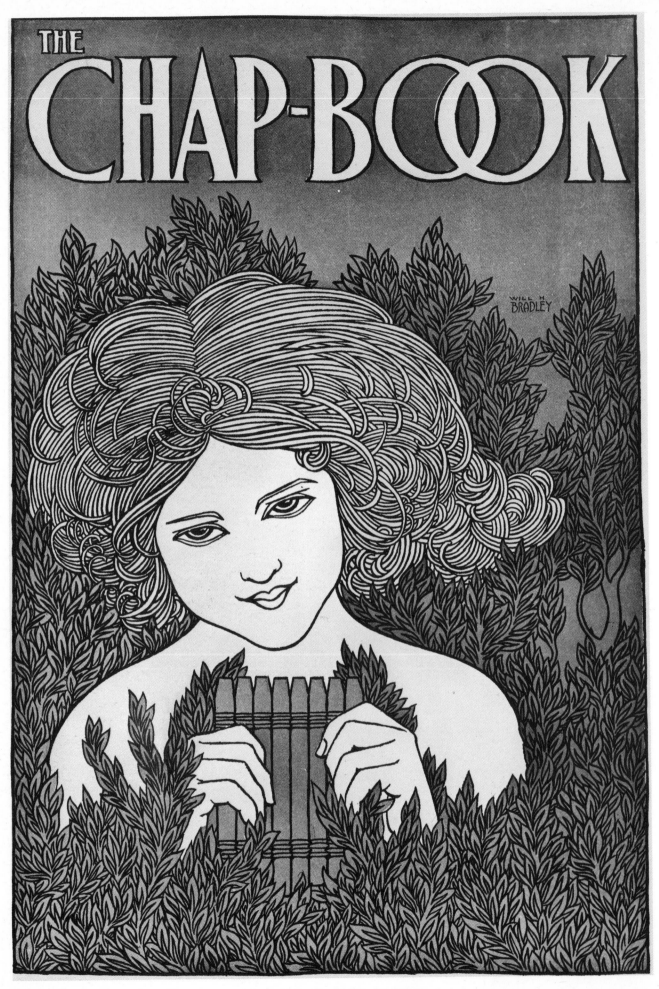

William H. Bradley 1895 21 x 14in

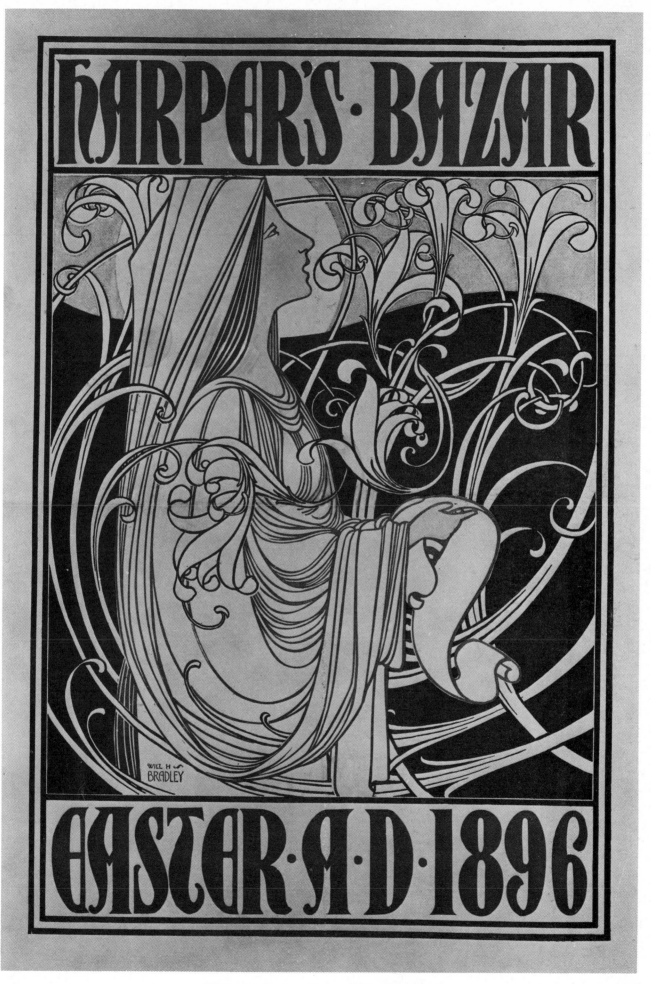

William H. Bradley  Easter 1896  15.5 x 11in

William H. Bradley  c.1895  22.5 x 14.5in

40

# The Chap-Book

William H. Bradley  1894  20 x 14in

William H. Bradley  1895  17.5 x 14in

WHEN HEARTS
ARE TRUMPS ♥
BY TOM HALL

William H. Bradley  1890  16.5 x 13.5in

L.N. Britton  1917  31 x 23.5in

Claude Fayette Bragdon  c.1896  21 x 13.5in

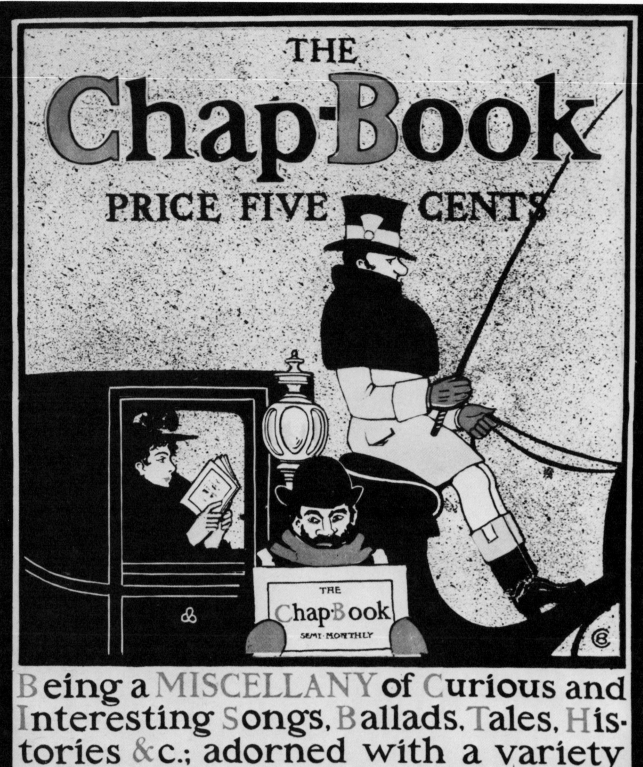

Claude Fayette Bragdon  c.1896  18.5 x 12.5in

THE NAVY IS CALLING
ENLIST NOW

U.S. NAVY RECRUITING STATION

L.N. Britton  39 x 25.5in

# KEEP HIM FREE

BUY **W.S.S.** WAR SAVINGS STAMPS ISSUED BY THE UNITED STATES GOVERNMENT

# WAR SAVINGS STAMPS
## ISSUED BY THE UNITED STATES TREASURY DEPT.

Charles Livingston Bull  17.5 x 18.5in

# SCRIBNER'S

# FOR NOVEMBER
# NOW READY PRICE 25 CENTS

Blendon Reed Campbell  1903  21.5 x 14in

William L. Carqueville  c.1895  19 x 14in

William L. Carqueville c.1890 19 x 14in

Howard Chandler Christy  1917  37.5 x 24.5in

Eugenie De Land 1917 28.5 x 18.5in

THE

# BOOKMAN

MAY
number
price
20
cents

MDCCCXCVI

DESIGNED·FOR·THE·BOOKMAN·BY·GEORGE·WHARTON·EDWARDS·1897·

George Wharton Edwards  May 1897  16 x 10.5in

Casper Emerson Jr.  29 x 19in

Charles B. Falls  39 x 27in

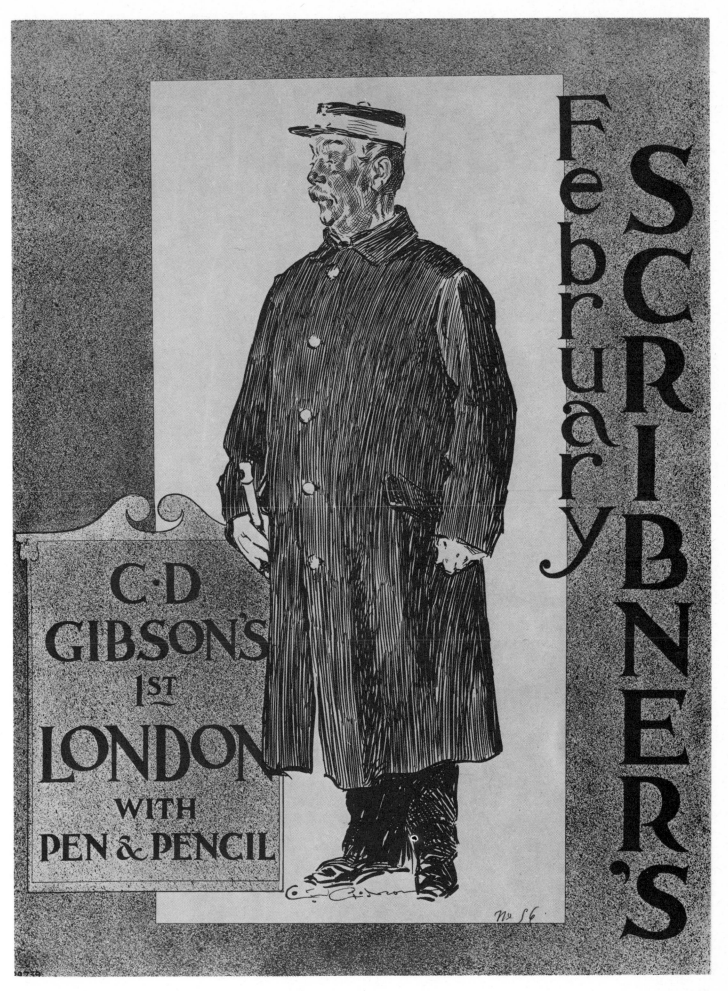

Charles Dana Gibson c.1899

Alice R. Glenny  30 x 21.5in

J.J. Gould  November 1896  17 x 12in

J.J. Gould  March 1897  17 x 14in

# U. S. NAVY

"Here he is, Sir."
We need him and you too!
Navy Recruiting Station

Charles Dana Gibson  38 x 25in

Joseph Christian Leyendecker  29 x 19in

Maxfield Parrish  August 1897  20 x 14in

Edward Henry Potthast  1895  38.5 x 29in

J.J. Gould  April 1897  16.5 x 12.5in

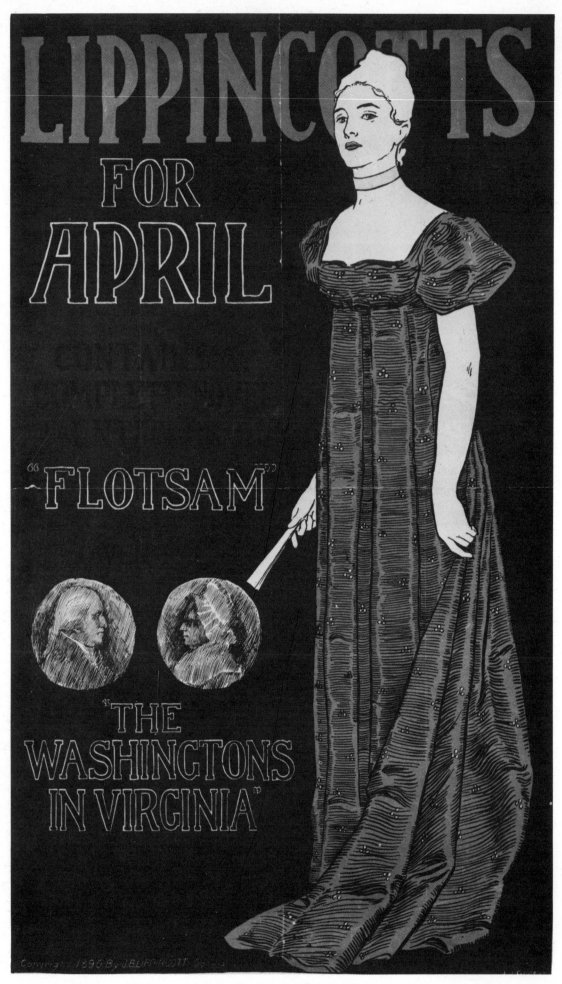

J.J. Gould  April 1896  33 x 15in

Frank Hazenplug 1895 20.5 x 14in

L.F. Hurd  c.1895  15 x 10in

Joseph Christian Leyendecker   August 1896   21.5 x 16in

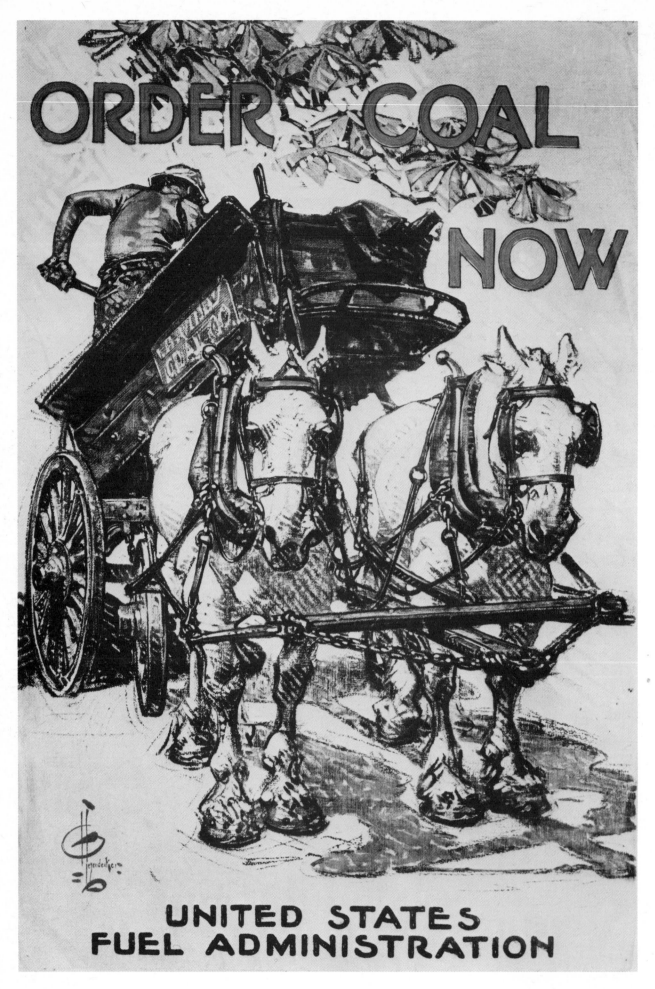

Joseph Christian Leyendecker  29 x 20in

Joseph Christian Leyendecker  19.5 x 14.5in

Florence Lundborg  c.1896  19.5 x 14.5in

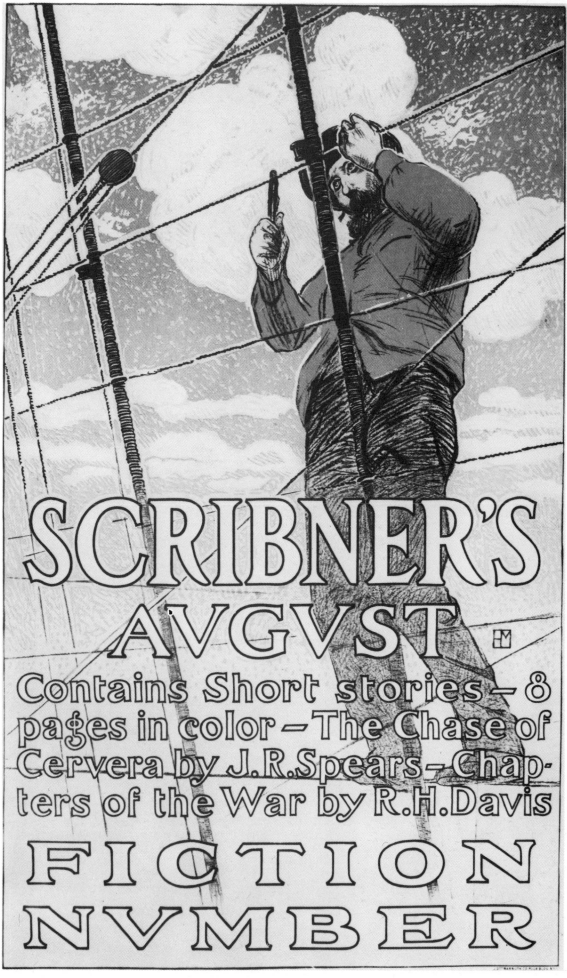

Henry McCarter  23.5 x 13.5in

Blanche McManus (Mrs Francis Milton Mansfield)  1895  20.5 x 14.5in

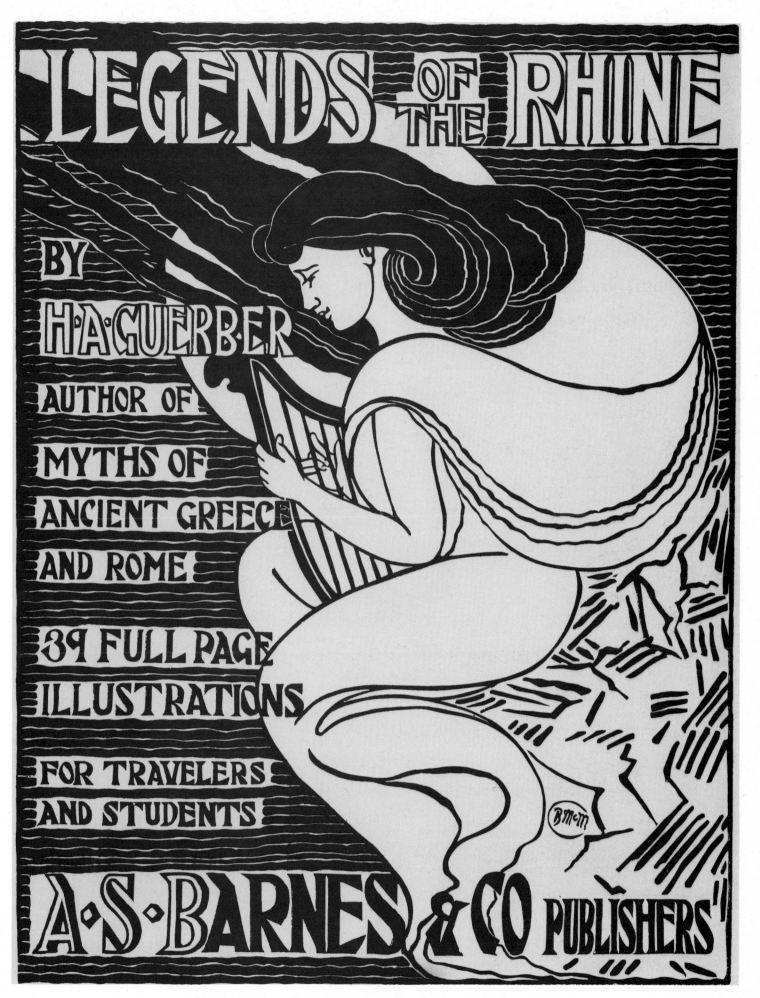

Blanche McManus (Mrs Francis Milton Mansfield) 1895 20.5 x 15.5in

Blanche Ostertag  before 1908  20 x 13.5in

Blanche Ostertag  19 x 13in

Maxfield Parrish  18 x 12in

Edward Penfield  May 1895  17 x 13.5in

Edward Penfield  August 1895  18.5 x 12in

Edward Penfield  c.1896  17.5 x 11.5in

Edward Penfield  June 1896  18.5 x 14in

Edward Penfield  July 1896  18.5 x 14in

Edward Penfield c.1896 17.5 x 11.5in

Edward Penfield  c.1896  17.5 x 11.5in

Edward Penfield  April 1897  14 x 14.5in

# HARPER'S 1897

### THE JANUARY NUMBER CONTAINS

White Man's Africa, by POULTNEY BIGELOW.
—The Martian, by DU MAURIER.—Farce, by
W.D. HOWELLS.—Short Stories, by Miss WIL-
KINS, BRANDER MATTHEWS, and E. A. ALEX-
ANDER.—Science at the Beginning of the
Century, Illustrated.—Literary Landmarks
of Rome, by LAURENCE HUTTON, etc., etc.

Edward Penfield  January 1897  18 x 13.5in

Edward Penfield 1910 29 x 20in

"THE First Gentlemen" of this Country wear our clothes *as illustrated in the new* WASHINGTON NUMBER *of* The Style Book *ready* March 1st

Hart Schaffner & Marx
*Good Clothes Makers*

Edward Penfield  28.5 x 19.5in

Joseph Pennel  32 x 27in

# SCRIBNER'S

# FOR FEBRUARY
# NOW READY PRICE 25 CENTS

James Preston  February 1904  22 x 14.5in

# SCRIBNER'S

# FOR SEPTEMBER
# NOW READY PRICE 25 CENTS

James Preston  September 1904  22 x 14in

Ethel Reed  1895  17.5 x 9.5in

Louis John Rhead  Christmas 1894  19.5 x 13.5in

Louis John Rhead  1895  16.5 x 10in

Louis John Rhead 1896 46 x 58.5in

Louis John Rhead  1895  44 x 24in

Louis John Rhead  1896  21 x 11in

Louis John Rhead  1894  43.5 x 25.5in

Louis John Rhead  1896  22 x 16.5in

Louis John Rhead  Christmas 1895  19.5 x 13.5in

101

Hazel Roberts  24 x 18in

# AINSLEE'S

The Islands of the Pacific THE WORLD'S TELEGRAPH The Indian Congress OUR CONGRESSIONAL PRESIDENT

Short stories by OPIE READ BRAND WHITLOCK NORMAN DUNCAN

Continued story by BRIG. GEN. CHARLES KING Poems, Illustrations, etc.

APRIL

ALL NEWS-DEALERS·TEN CENTS

Mark Rutherford  April 1900  18 x 13in

# U.S. MARINES
## FIRST TO FIGHT FOR DEMOCRACY
### ENLIST AT

L.A. Shafer 1917 34.5 x 25.5in

Moods

An Illustrated
Quarterly
for The Modern

Published by
The Jenson Press
Philadelphia, U. S. A.

John Sloan  1895  19 x 11in

Penrhyn Stanlaws (Penrhyn Stanley Adamson)  1900  24.5 x 13.5in

Albert Edward Sterner 1918 36 x 28in

CENTURY

MAY

Robert J. Wildhack  1908  21.5 x 14.5in

Robert J. Wildhack  21.5 x 14.5in

Robert J. Wildhack  23 x 15in

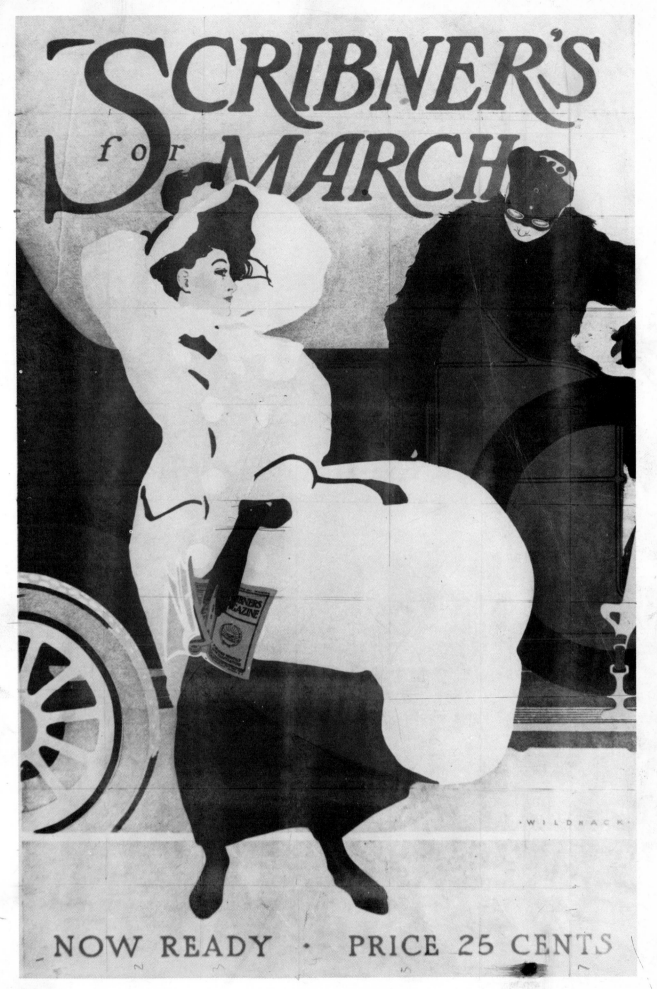

Robert J. Wildhack  23 x 12.5in

Charles Herbert Woodbury  July 1895  18.5 x 11in

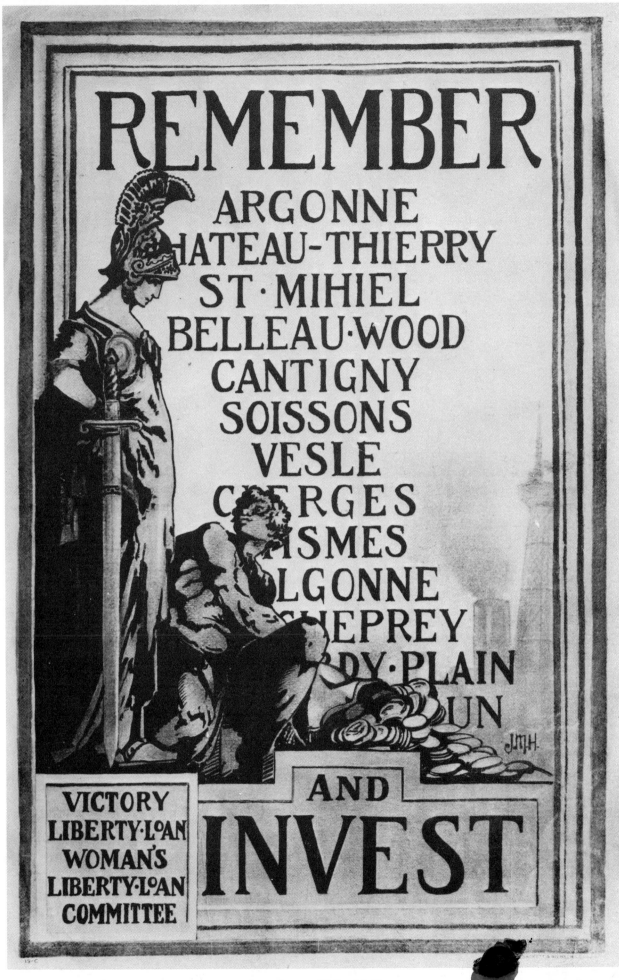

Anonymous  28.5 x 18.5in

Anonymous  1901  47.5 x 25in

Anonymous  c.1918  21.5 x 17.5in

# Bibliography

American Federation of Arts, *The American Poster,* New York 1967.

Alexandre, Arsène, H.C. Bunner, M.H. Spielmann and August Jaccaci, *The Modern Poster*, New York 1895.

Bradley, William H., *Will Bradley, his Chap Book*, New York 1955.

Breitenbach, Edgar, *The Poster Craze; the American Heritage*, New York 1962.

*British & Colonial Printer & Stationer*, July 1896. 'Anglo-American Poster Art'.

*Century Magazine*, July 1912. 'A Master of Make-Believe' by Christian Brinton.

Connolly, L., *Posters and American War Posters, historical and explanatory*, Newark 1917.

Hardie, Martin, *War Posters 1914-19*, London 1920.

Hiatt, Charles, *Picture Posters*, London 1895.

Hillier, Bevis, *Posters*, London 1969.

*100 Years of Posters*, London 1972.

Hornung, Clarence P. (Ed.), *Will Bradley, His Graphic Art*, New York 1974.

Jones, Sydney R., *Posters and their designers*, London 1924.

Kauffer, E. McKnight, *The Art of the Poster*, London 1924.

Ludwig, Coy, *Maxfield Parrish*, New York 1973.

*Les Maîtres de l'Affiche*, 5 volumes, Paris 1896-1900.

Malhotra, Ruth and Christina Thon, *Das frühe Plakat in Europa und den USA: Ein Bestandskatalog*, Berlin 1973.

*Das Plakat*, Charlottenburg, Berlin 1920.

Pollard, Percival (with an introduction by Edward Penfield), *Posters in Miniature*, London 1896.

*The Poster*, 4 volumes, London 1898-1900.

Price, C. Matlack, *Posters—a critical study*, London 1913.

*Poster Designers*, New York 1922.

Rickards, Maurice, *Posters of the First World War*, London 1968.

Rogers, W.S., *A Book of the Poster*, London 1901.

Sheldon, Cyril, *A History of Poster Advertising*, London 1937.

*The Studio*, London.

Vries, Leonard de, and Ilonka van Amstel, *The Wonderful World of American Advertising 1865-1900*, New York 1972.

# Index

Page numbers printed in *italics* refer to pages on which illustrations appear.